This anthology features winning entries from an annual competition which is free to enter. Winners also receive a free copy of the anthology. If you would like to enter, send a first class stamp and three poems, each of 20 lines and 160 words maximum, to Byword, 1 Yorke Street, Burnley, BB11 1HD.
You can also call us on 01282 459533 or visit our website on byword.net
Byword is a division of United Press Ltd

National Poetry Anthology 1999

Contents

Each poet listed in this contents of the National Poetry Anthology is a winner in his or her own right. These poems have been selected as winners for their town or area in a free-to-enter annual competition which featured many thousands of entries. The winners are grouped into various regions. If you do not find a winner from your locality this is because insufficient entries were received from that area.

EAST MIDLANDS - Page 51

Lorraine Trueman, Nottingham, David Crossland, Ripley, John Woolley, Arnold, Mary Waters, Spalding, Sally Spedding, Northampton, Andrew Fletcher, Hucknall, Andrew Starsmore, Corby, Gill Whyman, Leicester, Helen White, Skegness, Jay Baker, Grantham, Sandie Bowers, Louth, Sarah Lawson, Lincoln, Anne Harvey, Oakham.

EAST ANGLIA - Page 60

Andrea Grimes, Newmarket, Charlotte Allum, Felixstowe, Eric Swann, Norwich, Graham Dunn, North Walsham, Nicola Scott, Bury St Edmunds, Peter Buckingham, Cambridge, Laurence Calvert, Gt Yarmouth, Richard Reeve, King's Lynn, Rosalyn Tortice, Cromer, Tim Morgan, Colby.

NORTH WEST - Page 68

Anne Clare, Todmorden, David Walker, Nelson, Edmund Bradbury, Wilmslow, Jessica Pritchard, Warrington, Anne McTavish, Ulverston, Caroline Peate, Runcorn, David Holland, St Helens, Joyce Sugarman, Winsford, Jean Turner, Preston, Joan Kelly, Prestwich, Joyce Leigh, Bury, Marian Smith, Whitehaven, Paul Roberts, Kirkby, Rita Sheldon, Lancaster, Robert Fraser, Burnley, Terry Coneys, Chorley, Susan Hindley, Chester, Carmel Allison, Thornton Cleveleys, Eunice Lee, Wigan, Janet Owens, Liverpool.

NORTH EAST - Page 83

Alice Longley, Wakefield, Ashleigh Fletcher, Sunderland, Brian Denton, Morpeth, Carol Stubbs, Bridlington, Cathy Chadwick, Mexborough, E Lawson, Pontefract, George Thomas, South Shields, James Wilkinson, Harrogate, Jean Oxley, Scarborough, Jim Cuthbert, York, Joan Firth, Pudsey, Leigh Arkwright, Barnsley, Mary Found, Knaresborough, Vonny Holloway, Sheffield, Matthew Norcliffe, Skipton, Philip Cook, Ripon, Saiqah Salim, Bradford, Sheila Gannon, Leeds, A Gillmeister, Selby.

SCOTLAND - Page 96

Bill Chapman, Dumbarton, Dorothy White, Clydebank, James Watt, Aberdeen, Scott Martin, Dundee, Thomas Bell, Glasgow, W Winton, Edinburgh.

Foreword

Welcome to our first annual National Poetry Anthology.

The anthology is totally unique in the world of poetry and has been created to encourage new poetry talent. Poets from all over England, Scotland and Wales were invited to submit samples of their work and, from these, our judges at Byword selected winners for each area.

The anthology was far more successful than we anticipated and we were able to select a large number of winners. However, work on the next anthology has already begun and we anticipate that the response will be even greater and we will be able to select twice as many winners. The one thing that makes the anthology totally unique and also, at the same time, extremely attractive to budding poets is that it is free to enter the competition and all entrants are allowed to submit three poems, instead of just one, which is the norm for poetry competitions. Not only this, each winner receives a free copy of the anthology which includes his or her poem.

The millennium edition of the book has been widely advertised and promoted. In fact, we have donated almost £10,000 worth of copies of this year's book to the media. This increased publicity can only improve the anthology and further increase its credibility as truly representative of new poetry talent. I sincerely believe the anthology will go on to become even more established as a yardstick for poetic achievement. It is something which all new poets can turn to for inspiration and also look upon as an opportunity to achieve recognition as serious writers.

Finally, I cannot complete this foreword without thanking all the poets who helped to make this book such a success.

Peter Quinn, Editor.

This anthology featuring the work of poets from
England, Scotland & Wales

ISBN 1-902803-02-7

First published in Great Britain in 1999 by
BYWORD
1 Yorke Street
Burnley
BB11 1HD
Tel: 01282 459533
Fax: 01282 412679
Website: byword.net

*Cover photo by courtesy of
North West Tourist Board*

Byword is a division of United Press Ltd

South
East

HAPPY HOLIDAY

The Sky is blue - but not me too -
my deck-chair's in its station
and never fear - now Summer's here
that I am on vacation.
The seagulls mew - there's quite a few
and one that's getting portly
But never fear - the time is near -
the pubs will open shortly
The tide is out - the children shout
a couple of them weeping
but never fear - I shall not hear -
I'll be too busy - sleeping
My shoes and socks are by the rocks
my jacket within paces
but never fear - at all my dear
I'm keeping on my braces
The sun is hot and like as not
my head will burn and frazzle
but never fear - my hanky here
will stop some of the dazzle
This is the best - my annual rest
ABROAD? that's fiddle faddle, -
and never fear - the water's near
I go in for a paddle.
The rain - you frown - is coming down
and so it is by JINGO -
But never fear - I'm off from here
to find a game of bingo.

Don Kenny, Baldock

PAUL, A YOUNG MAN

Paul was a man
With a heart of gold
He lived with his mum
Who was really old

He drove a rusty banger
That was constantly for sale
And in the back was a blanket
With a curious smell

He liked the great big T.V.
In the corner of the lounge
And late at night he'd watch the porns
But with the volume turned right down

He'd get up late each morning
And gulp down his tea
And as he'd leave his mum would wave
To say bye to this MP

Anna Sexton, Milton Keynes

PASS THE PARCEL

The Golden Eagle Pub looked inviting
We stepped in my daughter and I,
It invited us without saying a word,
The smell was rich
And the crowded bar was like a
large living turtle
It swayed on the carpet
The Juke box shook its neon lights,
It had all the richness of home
With comfortable seats and thin
legged bar stools
Large mirrors reflected

Large bosomed bar-maids
Then I noticed the passing of
the parcel
So innocently done,
From hand to hand
The packet so white
Retreating figures thro' the door,
Only to be followed by the plain-clothes detective.
Trained for observance
Trained for swift movement
My daughter and I continued
sipping our drinks
Each reaching the same conclusion -
Passing the parcel is no game.

Irene Arnold, Southsea

WAITING FOR THE SMELL OF RAIN

The taste of air is sour with heat;
Flat sky unwraps, unfurls, unrolls.
I think of you; perhaps some neat
Cliche about your broken souls

Own storm-clad life with clouded skies
Beyond and gathering all around
To cover humid silent cries
And smother all the endless ground
Between us.

For unknown time you watch the cloud
For heavy rolling skies to burst.
Unknown by you I cry aloud
To storms unseen, to break the worst

Oppressive skies. I know I will
In wretched heat cry out again -
But evermore I find you still,

Still waiting for the smell of rain

James Clark, Bracknell

THOUGHTS ON FLYING

I've booked the tickets, so I know I am going
To America. Oh what am I doing!
You will enjoy it the children all say
You sit and relax and have meals on a tray
It's just like being at home, so they've found.
But I know it is not, I'm faraway from the ground!
Take plenty to do such as puzzles and books
And even some knitting - you won't get funny looks.
It can be quite boring, says our most travelled son,
Seven hours in a plane is not his idea of fun.
But nevertheless it has to be done
If we want to see our youngest grandson.
When I see the planes high up in the sky
I do wish that I did not have to fly
But I've booked the tickets, so I know I am going
To America. Oh What am I doing!

M Norman, Gosport

HARRY'S BIRTHDAY

Today is Harry's Birthday
Much to our delight
We know he's very busy
On his computer every night

Sometime ago there was another man
They called him Robert Burns
In fact his birthday also landed on
the 25th of Jan

He was clever with his words
And used the mighty pen

I bet he wished he had a computer
Waiting in his den.

The moral of this story
Is that Harry's having fun
Working out those solutions
That drive us round the bend.

Margaret Diana Barker, Basingstoke

AFTER LI BAI

Here, the waterfall
Becomes astral,
Star on star

Centuries.
Centuries.
Love, and be still.

I picture these roses
As a kind of radiant
Red snow

The endless shadow
Of a Japanese
Kiss

The haiku is holy
As the dream
Of a bee.

Anthony Marcoff, Epsom

IN WILLINGDON CHURCHYARD

A Garden of Remembrance,
Two small slabs, side by side.
So many years have passed away

Since these three people died.
'Fifty-seven and 'fifty-eight
And nineteen sixty-one,
Their lives were over, whereas mine
Had barely just begun.
I read the names, try to recall
Each face, each voice - but no;
An overwhelming sadness, realising
It's too long ago.
Granny, Grandad, Uncle Bill,
Part of my family,
But part of my past, a distant past,
A vague, dim memory.

Weatherworn words on weatherworn stone
Are all that now remain....
Except for a faded sepia print
In a battered silver frame.

Angie Creed, Eastbourne

DREAM GARDEN

In my dream garden flowers bloom all year round.
Grass stays even and green.
There is no need to till the soil.
And weeds are never seen.

In my garden there are no nasty bugs.
No fungus on the trees.
There are no aphids, ants or slugs.
Only butterflies and bees.

All kinds of vegetables grow in my patch.
With fruit throughout the year.
I grow roses no gardener can match.
With no nasty thorns to fear.

I wake up, and on reflection,
I think I'd miss the spring.
I couldn't live with such perfection.
No fun without the sting.

My garden stays as nature would have it.
With good and bad all together.
I will still hoe it and weed it.
And love it whatever the weather.

Eileen Root, Colchester

ARM'S LENGTH

Don't alter my senses
Just push me away.
I don't want to smell the sweet scent of your affection
As I'll just lose you someday.

Don't try to win me
I don't want to be won.
You won't learn to really hurt me
If we are over, before we are begun.

Don't try and understand with your hollow empathy
I don't want to let you near, or to let you see me.
The way to make the lady happy is to make her feel
That she's a classy catch so proudly reel in you reel.

If the words I spoke were the thoughts in my head
You'd want me out of your life, not into your bed.

Frances Easter, Whitstable

THE SOLOIST

Crafted like a fine Stradivarious,
I play second-fiddle to none.
My strings are tuned to wind and waves,

the purest music under the sun.

I play for the one Great Conductor,
with strings that are often strained.
By callous hands which have plucked them,
until timbre is cracked, veneer stained.

I play with a flourish, as I am conducted,
after each interlude.
The signature that best inspires me,
slow tempo, harmonic mood.

I strive, in concert, for harmonisation,
but not at the cost of my soul.
For I will not give up my soloist's chair,
until that final drum-roll.

The maestro knows of my discords,
as well as my best symphony.
My finest composition, He beckons with
Baton, play that as the finale.

Gordon Read, Orpington

AFTER LUNCH

Sunlight crowns the second sister
aureole of gilded hair
dancing the sea shore
in celebration of life and sorority.
A light breeze, a wisp of something
more substantial,
sharing an afternoon with us,
before other luminaries
pull her back
to another life.
Her laugh lingers,
a perfect cadence.

A flourish of chrome and red paint
completes today's performance.
Exit our heroine, stage right.

Hildi J Mitchell, Brighton

QUARRY

I scratched his hand by accident
"God - I'm sorry!" I yelled
my own hand at my mouth in reflex.
But there wasn't any of the blood that I expected
only a glint of pink granite
that winked at me through the pale torn skin.
Heart sinking - I guessed then
that beneath this warm exterior -
if I dug deeper -
I'd find a heart of stone.

J A Karpinska, Hove

FROST LIGHTS

Ripped page, broken-down book
leave my mind to wander undefiled;
Life's erudite jaunts now as at the start,
and still undigested.
Death, the last great chapter
flipped over and covered up.
Make no reference to noble learning -
human brain cannot fathom brain matter,
or know of the beginning's pulse,
still less those endless gelid years.
Track the orbital space,
clear the meaning -
Glass mirrors of the soul together,
I see you with frost lights
in your eyes.

Patricia A Morris, Romsey

THE DUNGENESS CAT

The fishermen are my friends,
I wait for them on the shore;
the winds blowing my fur
and I hear the sound of the rolling waves.

What will they catch today for me?
something tasty for my tea.
Flounders, Dabs, Plaice and Huss or a special treat of
Mackerel.
My little pink tongue waters, as the boats come to shore.

There are thirty fishing boats at Dungeness,
so I know I will not starve,
they're very kind to their ginger cat;
they see me waiting patiently for them on the shingle
shore.

Jasmine Bates, Folkestone

ENDURANCE TEST

Gathered light of days gone by.
Fragmented moments that are lost.
Memories of once that was.
Half captured in the now that is.
Where has it gone?
Merciful Time? Relentless Time?
Will all be revealed
Of days gone by?
Will it all screen before my eyes?
Or will I find-to my relief
That Merciful Time has paid the score
And power has gone from
Days gone by.
Will all be revealed of days gone by?
Will it all screen before my eyes?

Whose cloak will shield the agony?

Kathleen Bailes, Lewes

MY PARADE

I am an ocean that runs so deep
I am the water to cleanse your feet
I am the tree to give you shade
I was made for you to walk on, be my parade

Wherever you've been, I've held your hand
Whenever you've fell I've softened your land
Run to me and I will heal your wounds
For I am an ocean that runs so deep
I am the water to cleanse your feet
I am the tree to give you shade
I was made for you to walk on...come be my Parade.

Marina O'Shea, Basildon

DIRTY TEETH

Phil's mum was extremely keen
To keep his peggies sparkling clean,
A daily brush my little lad
Will keep your teeth from going bad.

As he got older, though he knew
This so important thing to do,
He always seemed in too much rush
To give his teeth the slightest brush.

Small cavities appeared, then grew,
Teeth snapped off, first one, then two,
Until at last, those who were closest,
Told him he had halitosis.

The dentist said, it was quite clear

Neglect had given him pyorrhea;
There is, I am afraid, no doubt,
I'll have to take the whole lot out.

Phil now keeps his false teeth clean
With Steradent and abscess cream
And often thinks when home alone,
It would be nice to have his own.

Michael J Morton, Faversham

THE EYE

This world is shaped, uncoloured
Save for the magic of the eye,
Translating varied rays of white
Into rainbow's glory bright,
As light alights.

Lo! This small orb
Clothes that huge sphere
With wonder and delight,
Bequeathing hues to sight
As light alights.

Vast symphonies of blue;
An infinity of greens;
Spectrum's blaze 'twixt day and night
Pours from the instrument of sight
As light alights.

Michael Sawyer, Hastings

FOR YOU

How gorgeous to feel the feminine touch
A velvet pour, a look of lust
A time to love and take the day

Lift aching heart with angels sway
When mindless thoughts just seem to wane
And flickers of fun take centre stage
To free this soul of pain and fear
If only for a time so clear
I long for this to be eternal
Where life is beyond a dream
I believe in this passion a passionate time
Am I the only one I cry?

Ty Germaine, Ashford

TUNNEL OF LIFE

Dry those tears,
Consider the years,
You've ambled and scrambled
Down life's tenuous way,
Now you are able to say
I've lived!

Living's a potent overture
Of sadness and hope
That fate and her orchestra play
at a slow mesmerising lope.

Sometimes, distracted, we get out of step,
mishearing a beat.
But fate commands strife
To restore our feet
To the rhythm of life:
Nature's heartbeat!

Yolande Clark, Clacton on Sea

MALAISE - IN LATE OCTOBER

Days of grey
that lately stay.
Seldom sun: one single ray,
as searching winds lurch and stray.

Colder, where this air you breathe.
Hurries by, so simply leave;
searching out, to clutch and thieve.
Wet wood and thicket rise and heave,
wherever unseen breath may weave.

All in obeyance are easy prey.
Subject to rancour and decay.
Leaves lie: little, where they lay,
in lane, field, fold, or bridleway.

Around homes, wild winds still drone and roam
as Autumn's gown is long outgrown,
which all these wicked winds have thrown:
to leave her destitute, -alone.
With time 'twill all be unbeknown!

Prone lie leaves by laundered gown
A few late-leavers, flurry down.......

Brian Stevens, Winchester

VAMPIRESS

Butter haired Sue
Was once my friend.

Raspberry cheeked
Beautiful clear eyed Sue.

A fresh cream scone of a girl.

She gave me clothes,
Encouraged me to go out and about,
Constantly seeking my company.

Gregarious, hilarious Sue.

But then she started eating me.
The more voracious,
The more vivacious she became.

I began to fade away,
And when I'd gone,
Sue found someone else unhappy
Who she could feed upon.

Val Rice, Maidenhead

South
West

JUST READ IT

Witches and warlocks, pixies and elves
Fairytale books found on children's shelves
Mythical dragons and unicorns
Or mathematics in its various forms
Charts of the planets and stars you can see
Atlas to learn about geography
Sketch of a flower so real you can smell it
Dictionary showing you just how to spell it
Poetry and prose, or musical score
Fictional, factual, novels galore

When to prune roses or Do It Yourself
The answers are found on a library shelf
And all about nature, tornadoes and hail
Visually impaired? You'll find it in Braille
Physics or politics, something to mend?
Computers and graphics, an E Mail to send?
Information is there whenever you need it
Education you want? Then just read it
IN A BOOK.

Freda Baxter, Bournemouth

BANA

Sweet scored calloused muscles
Made corded by labour of life
Clothed belt worn at his ankle
Now absent of his knife;
that trusted friend who had grown weary
lay broken on Mendip Rock
Among the fleeing memories
Where jackdaws clustered to mock

They came at night in three ships

Of inland seas not made to sail
They came among the darkness
and sentries choose to fail
for to light the beacons that were made
To guard the lonely tribe
Now all remained, was dust and pain,
Of promises that had died

As his tears sheltered the ground
A stream took for its own
The water running from this life
through pastures and flowers grown
wild by care of Nature's tendering
And, there, within his death
the River gathered in a pool
to give vision, peace and rest

A Church now stands over his well,
but still the waters flow
Not time, nor age, nor centuries
Will make its rhythm slow
nor cease such gentle melody
that Bana plays there at your side
A guiding light before your face
Of a gift that will ever survive.

Carol Wood, Weston-Super-Mare

EVENING

Evening shadows cross the land,
Fashioned by the Master's hand.
Twilight closes summer day,
Softer now, the breezes play.
Muted colours take the eye
Far swathed across the darkening sky.
See, song-birds resting on the bough,

Their busy day is over now.
Cattle low in shrouded mist
Whilst field and hedgerow mingle, kiss.
Vesper bells sound far away,
They summon faithful "Come and pray.
Guard and keep us 'till the dawn,
'Till the miracle of morn.
Save us from the fears we dread
Whilst we slumber in our bed."
Pink and purple flood the sky,
Night is coming by and by.
So stark the tree upon the hill....
Silence. All the world is still.

John Trembath, Newquay

WORMS

Horror of its muteness,
Soft simplicity
in a dark world
of jaws and impulse.

Destined for the gut.
Condemned to grow.
Swollen on a bitter diet
Of urgency.

The found, the eaten.
Grubs of gluttony
Chewing magnolia buds,
restless and fat.

Preyed upon in turn,
an incidental victim
abandons its skin
to suction.

Stripped veins
embellish the wind.

Michael Brandon, Taunton

LUCY

The stairs are twisted, the centre
Narrow. Lucy, beautiful Lucy, sits
On the wide, white window ledge, gazing
Down at her kingdom. Sat here,
On the wide edge, resting on her mantle, I'm
Secure. Brave now, I cry fearlessly
"How far do you dare me to go, Lucy?"
"I dare you, I dare you", a familiar game.

I inch my way towards the centre,
Narrow and narrower. Frozen suddenly
With fear, I cannot even cry out,
Just stare helplessly through the bars.
"I'm here" I slowly turn my head,
Lucy, serene, calm. Always here.

Ali Miller, Chard

SHELTER 2

Here sheltered from fine rain
which mentally hurts me
here hidden from the pain
that never now deserts me
Turnstones, gulls and seals
new-found seaside friends
- you know how it feels
when trust abruptly ends.
When rumours hurt like fire
and glances keep one at bay.
The overwhelming desire

to shelter here all day.

David Hart, Swindon

THE GATHERING

The morning light slips through the pane,
Tis hushed 'cept for a lark's refrain,
Down the hill and over the stile-
Around the lane in ragged file,
Walking together in ones and twos
To kneel and pray in oaken pews,
To breathe and chant in yellowed page,
As their fathers did in bygone age;
While siskins twitch on willowed brook,
Watched by the black-eyed gawky rook,
While swallows twist and wheel above,
Near the roost of the cooing dove;
While bluetits peck at pitted dung,
At the time the linnet's song begun;
While sparrows bathe on sandy bar,
Near to the crow with coat like tar
The cattle by the sheltered lea,
Lowing at the grassy sea.
The plover makes a plaintiff cry,
While churning up in the cloudless sky -
Life is such a precious thing,
Now, at last, the final hymn.

Geoffrey F Harrington, Bristol

NIGHT PROWL

Passing
Like a shadow
Unheeded
In the quick darkness
Moving
Beneath your window

Soundlessly
Unkempt
Watching
For your face
In the reflection
Of fallen teardrops
Listening
In the wind
For the rustling
Of your footsteps
Carrying your memory
Like unspent change
Rattling about
Dropping it at random
Like wishes in a well
Silently falling
Am I
From muted skies
Creeping
Among the gutter rats
And sighing
At the stars

Kirsten Aidan, Totnes

THE FLOWERY AFTERMATH

O, glory. O, delight,
The aftermath of the wedding.
Yellow and white,
Look where you're treading.
The flowers are all in buckets now,
All settled in a cosy row.
They're awaiting
Delivery to friends and neighbours,
And to liven up the church.
The arrangers bring scissors sharp as sabres.
No spray carnations are left in the lurch,

Nor any flower
In this resplendent, temporary bower
O glory, O delight,
My senses reel at such a sight.
An angel seems to be present,
Shedding celestial light
On earthly abundance.
These are fruits of His love,
Who attends from above
Our soul's needs to satisfy.
That, if we do sigh,
Its because of His grace,
Who is ever nigh,
Though hiding His face
Lest we should be overcome, and die
Before the presence of so much rich glory.

Ruth Bibby, Cheltenham

GRAN'S A SPORT

I couldn't wait to be a Gran,
All cuddly in my shawl.
I had a very special plan
where I'd be spoiled by all.

My Grandsons they would cherish me,
and stroke my silver hair.
They'd come around my house to tea,
and rock me in my chair.
It hasn't turned out quite to plan.
Good Gracious - Bless my soul.
All I hear is "Come out NAN, You're the next in GOAL!"

Betty Pledger, Torquay

BUT THIS IS AN EMERGENCY!!

Tell Dr Blood it's MRS BLOOMSBERRY;
He always sees ME right away;
He's such a wonderful doctor - so much
Better than that Doctor Gay!!

What the devil are you incinerating?
I consider your tone a right cheek!
I've not bothered you for AGES; I've
Not phoned for at least ... a week!

But this IS an emergency;
Yes of course it's SERIOUS,
I'm sweating, shivering, sneezing
And feel quite DELIRIOUS!

I'm running a terrible temperature,
I'm covered all over in spots,
My body aches from head to toe,
My muscles all tied up in knots.
My heart's got the palpitations,
Though I'VE STILL GOT A PULSE - it's quite weak;
My poor throat's ever so red and sore,
It's increasingly hard .. to ... speak!
My eyes are all glazed and weepy,
My ears are infected and blocked,
I think there's a chill in my kidneys
And my joints have all stiffened and locked.

My stools are alarmingly liquid,
My water's grey, misty and strong,
I'm suffering pins and needles, in fact ...
I don't think I'VE GOT VERY LONG!!

He can see me on Thursday morning?
An appointment for half-past-ten?

BUT THAT'S NO GOOD AT ALL TO ME ...
I'll be BETTER AGAIN - by then!!

Clive Blake, Wadebridge

ENLIGHTENMENT

The streetlamp knows the truth
But it will never tell.
It holds the secret of my love
And guards it very well.
The streetlamp saw it all,
That night you stole my heart,
Beneath its golden glow
You took me in your arms.
The streetlamp saw you kiss me
So very tenderly -
It knows what you were thinking:
But it cannot tell me.
The streetlamp saw you leave
Me on that starry night;
It watched you turn the corner
And disappear from sight.
The streetlamp heard me whisper
So quiet you did not hear -
Come back to me forever,
Your true love is right here.

Deborah Shepherd, Exmouth

NO DISTANCE APART

As I gazed far beyond that distant array
Bright light shone showering life all around you,
Such an elegant figurine full of spiritual warmth
Partially clothed in a fleece of golden cloud

Araised, came forth arms like wild eagle's wings

As if to guide me through, thus calming sorrow
You softly gathered my inner thoughts, expectant dreams
Hence raindrops became tears then crystallised my pain.

Calming breeze touches, timid your breath on my face
So fulfilled my feelings, a closeness that deepness hides
I could hear harmonised voices, hearts pounding within
Our souls entwined together, as one eternally bound.

Not just now but forever, we shall reminisce
Saluting our future, leaving present time with past
No more to feel loneliness, cruel sacrifice of loss
As our todays turn into yesterdays, 'No distance apart'.

Diana Bowden, Newton Abbot

PLEADING GUILTY

I'm sorry for the salt rubbed wound,
And vinegared broken heart.
My apologies for the wild horses,
That tore your life apart.
I'm sorry that I'm the damsel,
Who wouldn't let down her hair.
And I'm guilty of the harsh whispers,
That caused you such despair.
My guilt rides on the tidal wave,
That washed your love away.
And I'm sorry I caused you to love me,
In such an engulfing way.
I'm sorry that I'm the padded cell,
That drove you round the bend.
The only thing I do not regret,
Is that you've been such a wonderful friend.

Holly Cross, Bridgwater

LOVE SONG

When my love sings to me
he sings not in the dulcet voice
of tenor sweet or baritone
but in the sharpened
saw-edged
corncrake rasp
that renders down all candlelight
and soft-breathed words
into a tallow laced with grit
and yet
and yet
when my love sings to me
I feel the warmth
of seven thousand candles lit

Pamela Hodge, Plymouth

Wales

FUNNY MAN

Funny man that's what everybody calls me. Funny man.
Just because I stand on stage, make them laugh, or
make them rage. Yes Funny Man, Funny Man.
People say they envy me. Wish that they were as happy.
Yet inside there's nought to see. Inside this happy chappy.
Sometime ago I had romance. Turned it down, gave it no
chance. I was set and had a plan.
I was, going to be a Funny Man.
Funny Man, Funny Man. That's what everybody calls me
Funny Man. My sacrifice brought lots of money.
Heaps of praise from tongues of honey.
But now I'm old and a little grey,
He's not so funny now they say.

George Stephenson, Newport

JOURNEY IN TIME

There is a time machine in my house
It's called a clock of course
Though very often I have travelled in time
And by a really simple recourse

Whenever I feel like a journey in time
I turn that clock in my house to the wall
Then I get all my old photographs out
Very soon I am ready to recall

Those long ago happy, harmonious days
When there was laughter and joy everywhere
Life seemed to be a bed of roses,
Through which we wandered with nary a care

I look at the pictures I'd taken myself,
And all the ones taken of me,
With sighs of nostalgia when I go through them
As each one holds its own memory

Sighs quite audible, especially when sometimes
I have been brought close to tears
With remembering all of the happy times taking
those snaps, in the long ago magical years

When my journey is over I close my album,
Slowly return to the present day
Then I promise myself that very soon
I'll take another wistful time trip away.

Hal Takata, Cardiff

THE WILL TO SURVIVE

While sat fretting one day my attention was drawn to a rose
I wondered why in this world it chooses to live
Or why it so exuberantly grows
What is its purpose, What does it give?

The whiteness of its colour so bright
Opposes our outlook so grey
Its petals so tender and light
Yet life remains dense day after day

Carelessly it chases the warmth in the sun
As it tenderly caresses the breeze
It alters to cope with the damage to nature we've done
Every opportunity this rose will continue to seize

Persistently we moan and complain at every junction in life
Failure at every turnstile and all our decisions we fear
Unlike our ignorance the rose strives on strife
Even decapitation won't prevent its bloom next year!

Marie Gapper, Caerphilly

A DARK DREAM

Where Can I put this lonely love
up in the clouds maybe
If only I could reach
Where Can I send a broken heart
Along the path to heaven
If only I knew the way
Where is the Key to stop these tears
At the end of the rainbow
If only I could fly
Where Can I wash away the memories
In the sea of hope
If only it was deeper
Where oh where
Can I put an aching soul
to rest
In the hands of peace
If only I could Step
into my dreams.

Rebecca Punter, Bridgend

A DIFFERENT MORNING

This morning
a different sea, came
white crested to

crash upon the rocks.
No gentle lap,
no creeping stealth,
but wholehearted
full frontal
crashing spray
brought in high tide.
Whipped by cool breeze
the blue grey,
white coated sea rolled in.
A boisterous brother
to the gentle giant
that crept yesterday
so quietly.
Infinite faces
has this watery soul,
entrancing,
even mysterious!

Pat Rees, Abergavenny

West Midlands

GOBOWEN 1927

Snow flakes fell on the foot of the bed
The children lay still, wide eyed, black rimmed
Coughing, crying, young faces contorted in fright
The cold so intense many wet the bed

Nurses rushed round in their coats and scarves
Serving out diets of boiled fish, potatoes in skins
Coaxing and scolding, ensuring no one starved
Then the big spoon, its cod liver oil overflowing

The generators constant with their gentle humming
The clanging of metal jugs and bowls in the morning
Then the change in the storm that came in the night
With the rain and the hail on tin roofs drumming

Little eyes, from troubled minds, peeped out
For the wards had no walls to the sides and the front
What were they all thinking? Surely not of heaven!
Fresh air was the cure for TB in 1927

Albert R Lewis, Oswestry

POPPIES

A gentle sun that warms the body
Floats effortlessly across a tranquil sky
How peaceful and calm to watch those poppies
Playing in a tantalising breeze
Nodding courteously to one another
Friend and foe alike
How sad it is to remember
each poppy a soldier's soul
Or that of his unborn child
So much they gave

So much we take for granted
Do you think they know?
The lesson so costly taught
Was never really learnt

Andrew Perrett, Tupsley, Hereford

ALAN AND BILLY

Shearer, a striker in black and white stripes
No better than me in red, white and blue
Father says the media relate all his hypes
I don't get his cash, but I don't rue
I score class goals to reach my quantity
Without internationals Les, Peter and Phillip
Helped only by two brothers to show my quality
His three mates have played premiership

Teacher said I'll go to the top
You've scored fifty, he's only hit thirty
There's nothing to stop your annual crop
Keep your wrath under wraps, don't get shirty
Mother took my arm, I opened my eyes
You're dreaming Bill, I can tell by your sighs

Arthur Rice, Sutton Coldfield

A SUMMER'S DAY

The purple dawn is breaking in the cloudless eastern sky
Then with majesty and splendour the sun will slowly rise
Now it sheds it's golden sunbeams over meadow, vale and
sea
While the song-birds in chorus with a joyous melody

Let us wander through the gardens sloping down towards
the sea
And view the lovely flowers that attract the honey bee
Smell the fragrance of red roses growing round the cottage-
door
Hear the murmur of the sun-kissed waves rolling lazily to
the shore

Out in the quiet countryside soft breezes blow
Swaying gently through the cornfields where the wild red
poppies grow
Nearby we find a rippling brook that winds through leafy
glade
Where the slender silver-birch trees give a cool refreshing
shade

The summer day granted us is drawing to its close
Yet another joy awaits us before the night's repose
A pink and orange sunset, edged with gold and silver grey
Brings a fitting tribute to our God, and a perfect summer's
day

Doreen Irvine, Bromsgrove

LIVING IN A SILENT WORLD

I felt alone in a crowded room
I stood in a 'Silent World'
I didn't belong to the laughing crowd
I could only pretend that I 'heard'

I wanted to talk - just to join in
I enjoy being part of a team
But it's not so easy when people ask -
'What's that place like?'
And you don't even know if you've been

So you giggle and nod and vacantly smile
When they chat to each other you're 'glad'
You get up to leave, they call out your name
And you don't even hear them that's 'sad'

You hurry off home to your 'Silent Escape'
You're glad you pretend you heard
They're laughing out there - laughing out loud
But not in your 'Silent World'

June Sedgebear, Coventry

THE CITY OF STOKE-ON-TRENT
(PAST & PRESENT)

City smoke surrounds this place
A child plays with a dirty face
Dense, black clouds form in the air
But people here do not care

Colours fade as dust settles
Flowers may as well be nettles
Fresh air is what we are longing for
We must not tread dirt on the floor!
For this all makes the cleaning hard
Go outside and scrub in the yard

Look they've painted their gate black
No it's just the dirt from the track
Dirt and dust and fumes and waste
We can't keep up with the city's pace
Fresh air, clean air, country style
Is the escape for a little while

But that was in a time long past
Those conditions could not last

Now we have a city of bowers
Scented walks and colourful flowers

Mary Simpson, Stoke-on-Trent

THE MESSY DECEPTION

Cushioned in a sack of fluid buoyancy
In ignorance, I continue to slumber
Allowed to develop, in safe solitude
Unaware, of Mother's ungainly lumber

Gradually aware, the fit it is tighter
Of being manoeuvred, to ordained site
in here, still safe, but feel enormous
To those outside, I'm just a mite

Oh, there's a whoosh, my buoyancy gone
I'm wedged head first, if you please
So much pressure, pushed to and fro
Get on with it Mum, don't tease

At last, light, at the end of the tunnel
But what a time, it appears to be taking
Pushing, shoving and probing
Hey Mum, what a noise you are making

At last, I'm out, but just wait
I'm cold, sticky, I want to go back
Shall I scream, then the giants won't want me
Can I please return, to my safe, warm sack

Ooh, that's better, clean and dry
I'm warm, held by Mum, safe and snug
Soft kisses and sweet gentle words
"Hello Mum, do I look like a bug".

Theresa J Timlin, Leamington Spa

FIRE, FIRE

People stand
and sit and stare
at a vision of crimson
helpless and impaired

I see them, though
my eyes do not
As I see the flames
and the twisting pain
and I burn and writhe
in this living hell

My world came
Crashing down on me
in the house
Where it all began
Now I'm alone, in the darkness
with my memories and pain

Tanya Gould, Droitwich

SMILE PLEASE

Umbrellas bobbing up and down
Faces hidden from sight
Zig-zagging across a blackboard sky
Forked flashes of light
Children who are frightened
Wipe a tear from their eye
The flash is from God's camera
Taking photos in the sky
So if you wonder, why children
smile in the rain

It's because they are having a
photograph taken, again and again

Anne England, Hednesford, Cannock

TWISTED FATE

When I look at you
I see all too clearly
My own fate, my uncertain future

On this our wedding day
When I still ache to hollowness
With love, unconditional

When your blinking eyes
filmed with tears of devotion
take snapshots of our moment
And I make sure to smile

Before the film has been processed
And the two children we yearn for
Have screamed our love to silence

And your overexposed eyes
Have wandered and fixed on my image
Fresh and new but somehow different
Of ten years since

Victoria Minihane, Hollywood, Birmingham

WHERE ARE YOU NOW?

Where are you now?
Can you see us
Can you hear us

Do you know we are grieving
Where are you now?
Is there a heaven
Are there angels
Do they love you like we did
Where are you now?
We said goodbye today
Did you look down and watch
Could you see us crying
We hope you are happy -
Wherever you are now

Carol Somerfield, Rugby

SCRAP HEAP

Shining silver, coated mould
freckles brown that tingle cold
Peel of skin in a cankerous heap
Penetrating layers deep

Now met in shadows with hammer and tongs
No rest from fatigue and laboured wrongs
Once pure potential, design foresight
From molten mass speckled neon white

Bernard Pogson, Burton-on-Trent

East
Midlands

LISTEN WITH MOTHER

Could you honestly listen
to another's true confession,
without judgement;
without prejudice;
unbiased?
Would you willingly allow
another's voice
to be heard?
Would you lend an ear
to the inaudible,
to that which is not said?
Could you consciously listen
to yet another tale of woe,
without the urge to interpret;
without needing to understand;
undaunted?
Or are you deaf
to all but an echo
of your own internal thoughts
and fears?

Lorraine Trueman, Nottingham

FOOD

Boiled prawns carved kebab sheep
take-away orders rice with meat
fry-up cafe lunch-box larders
fast food fronts floodlit parlours
Kwik-Save staff neck-tied smart
pay-as-you-shop Co-op car park
Pizza hut on Bronte's cold land
food for thought by Sainsbury canned
washed fruit fine cuisine
request no fat only well-cooked lean

frozen fish oven ready fries
who cares if Coketown starving dies:
multiple-mix what does that matter
Ripley's head salad on a platter

David Crossland, Ripley

WITHIN NATURE'S REALM

I came across an unknown path
that time had bestowed to nature's tune,
The route was grassy and overgrown
and full of bluebells in sweetly tune.
I paused, then sat beneath the shade
of trees of every shape and cline,
A magnificent canopy, indeed admired,
This secret place I now then claim as mine.
No need to watch the hour of day
for time stands still, a much slower pace,
I listen intently, for many new sounds
are echoing around this beautiful place.
In solitude, and deep within nature's realm
peace and tranquillity rules the day;
Not that I had better things to do
or travel perhaps by some other way.

With sadness and regret I finally left that place,
As all good things eventually have an end;
I'll never divulge where nature and I were one,
I trust this secret dear reader will not offend.

John Woolley, Arnold

THE ASH TREE

Down the lane, the Ash tree now
Is clothed with green along the bough
Mature and graceful there it stands

Proud guardian of our ancient lands.
Pacific.

And I passed by today and saw
The splendour of the Ash once more
All hung with keys to signify
The unlocked ways beneath the sky.
Heraldic.

The tree of gold as well as green
Opening up the rural scene
Embracing all the fields nearby
That in its mighty shadow lie.
Symbolic.

Mary Waters, Spalding

NEWTON

The scent of lilac round the door
And evening primrose sweetening musk
Fill my memory and restore
The dream that darkens with each dusk.

Wild things once strewn about the dunes
By tides of wind made drily coarse,
And rabbits danced to unheard tunes
Amongst the salted yellow gorse.

No colour in my photograph,
And blurred the years of childhood's scene
Where now new children run and laugh,
And scuff the sand where I had been.

Sally Spedding, Northampton

THE TRAMP

The man shabbily dressed, steps into the road
Without looking, despair etched into every
filthy line on his face, eyes as empty as the
pockets on his torn and muddy coat.
The cold endless rain beats down from
A soulless sky, the man whose life is as empty
And pointless as the road he stands in doesn't
seem to notice, he turns his face up toward the
rain and blinks. I see him from time to time, this
unloved figure cutting against the grain of an
unloving city, endlessly wandering
Not for you this terrible scene of human agony
sketched in graphic detail for all to see on
living canvass. Some say vagrant, others with
impunity are more scathing still, and yet we do
not better ourselves if we condemn what we do not
care to understand, and if we dare not look upon
this caricature of neglect, then we stand
accused, and this man and me, we are not
so different after all

Andrew Fletcher, Hucknall

STATISTICS

A gun sounds its call of fate
In a split second, its target is found,
Her hand grabs mine in a obsolete,
Manner, as pain is the only sound.
This demonic man-made virus
Has entered her back, tearing
Her life away, oh God, why us?
Lying in my helpless arms, fearing
The separate lives now imposed
Upon us, in her brave face

I see all the reasons composed,
Of our undying love to face,
Nothing can tear us apart, in spirit
We will always be together, forever.
Tears flow more than blood, true grit
She shows, speaking words, so clever,
Distinctive of a mature dimension
That our thoughts do not comprehend.
Her soothing hand, with compassion
So deep, I let fall, I can't pretend,
As to what cannot be, I scream
It echoes in a tranquillised state
My loss is another statistic, I dream
Of a time when life is a valued estate.

Andrew Starsmore, Corby

A FEAST OF COLOURS

The fresh peas looked as black as coal,
the celery was pink
the meat it seemed to be quite grey,
I wonder what you think.
The lemons have turned orange,
the salad is sky blue
the milk it is a real blood red,
I'm not hungry now, are you?
The coffee's turning yellow
with nuts all scarlet red,
the eggs look blue and so do you,
let nothing more be said.

Gill Whyman, Coalville, Leicester

HANDS

A touch of a hand that covers yours
In a magic moment, a pause;

Hands can mean so much to you,
Hands can be so warm
Hands can turn a dark night
Into dawn.

An expressive hand can say so much
You only need to feel its touch.

Helen White, Skegness

HERBERT

Today James found Herbert the Hamster dead in Calum's room.
Where does the responsibility lie and with whom?
It was impossible for him to escape from his home and lair.
Am I supposed to drop in the depths of despair?
I would if Calum had found him, but that was not so,
And how the creature came there, I think I would rather not know.
I believe there are more than three predators, not of course the hound.
There is a mystery afoot and I know my suspicions are well found,
For the cage was quite intact.
There was no way he could escape from that.
Why? Why? I ask myself.
Was it a demon or a devious elf?

Jay Baker, Grantham

WHERE WE ARE

As autumn leaves fall from the trees
All around the landscape is bare
The swallows have flown to warmer climes
And my love you are not there

The cold winds blow round my heart
And leave me in utter despair
Now all is cold and dark and bleak
And my love you are not there

All winter long I can only dream
As I hibernate deep in my lair
By a cosy fire, but all alone
Because my love just isn't there

Tomorrow and tomorrow will dawn again
I'll waken and lay and stare
At the lonely walls in my empty room
For my love you are not there

Days pass by and time moves on
Oh how I need to share
My thoughts and hopes and joys with you
But still you are not there

You're far away whilst I am here
Reaching out to show I care
Through time and space in a world of dreams
But still you are not there

A new time for us will dawn
Life will be bright and clear
Then no more the pain of being apart
For not there my love, but here

Sandie Bowers, Louth

NATURE'S CANVAS

Nature gave us beauty
A paradise in which to learn
A relaxing peaceful setting
What did we give her in return

We didn't care for all her gifts
And encourage them to grow
We destroyed all that was in her path
halted the rivers' flow
We gave her cars and noise and smog
built tower block storeys high
Cut roads through her creations
Can't you hear her cry
What she gave was a canvas
Which she left for us to use
instead of painting life and peace
in many shades and hues
We painted death and sorrow
in different shades of grey
And with all our fears and problems
They'll grow darker every day

Sarah Lawson, Lincoln

MOMENTS

Standing, watching the rain, time slips by
The soothing sound fills your senses
The conscious mind relaxes its grip
Your thoughts drift away from the mundane
Dreams for your future to hold onto
There is a better world out there
Somewhere, for you to discover
The reality stifled for so long
The grey heavy clouds cover a sky -
So clear and blue, the brightness blinds
Hiding a perfect day -
That will come again -
For everyone to share

Anne Harvey, Oakham, Rutland

East
Anglia

DON'T DIE

I watch over you,
Wondering if this is the end,
You have been with me
For 5 1/2 years,
But I want many many more
With most of your energy drained
Is your life going as well?
How much more can I take
Before breaking point?
I dare not sleep
Afraid of what I will wake to
I listen to every cough and swallow,
Every breath is music to my ears,
Please don't stop
Not now
Not never

Andrea Grimes, Newmarket

MY FRIEND THE SEA

She's been beside me day by day - my lifelong friend the
sea
She knows my feelings, every mood, she helps and com-
forts me
She braces when I'm alone, she heals when I am sad
And when she tangles with the sun it helps to make me
glad

So when my hearts is troubled and life is far from kind
I need a listening quiet friend to tell what's on my mind
I walk there close beside her and feel she'll understand
And help me realise, alas, no one can take my hand

I love her when she's angry, when she heaves and puffs

and foams
She's grey and throws her spray, the seagulls soar and east winds moan
She's calm - and like a looking glass her colour turns to blue
her waves lap gently, gently, on the shore so near to you

Good things go on forever, far beyond this life we live
And love and nature friend outlast us all - when we forgive
So when my days are over and you need to search for me
You'll find me - dancing with the wind, on the shore beside the sea

Charlotte Allum, Felixstowe

HOT BOILER SWIM - HOLE AND SANDS

Every day I say I'll stay away,
But in the end, relent,
And visit you
Your brown, corrugated, golden thighs entice me
To wade to your green pubic weed.
Smiling small, white teeth crest;
And lure me to thrust deeper.
Then casting me aside,
Shrug off my advances,
With a nonchalant wipe-out wave.
You're in season!
You bitch!
Used by all men,
Sunnily ignoring my soliciting,
My private caressing.
Prostitute!
Wait 'till the north sea winter winds come,
And I'm your only late night caller;
Weaving on sodden steps,
And drunkenly peeing my name,

On your cold heartless face.
If I warm you,
I'll nonchalantly dot the "I"
Turn away-
And refuse to be patronised.

Eric Swann, Norwich

LEAVE THE LITTER

Leave the litter until the summer
When all the weeds are green and lush
When road and riversides overgrown
With verdant sward and leafy bush
Then all the rubbish - save a bit outstanding
Can be ignored - since hardly seen
And litter picking can be peripheral
The garbage hidden neath floral green

Better that than be particular
Better not to clear up all
Since if there be no longer litter
How will one justify the call
To be careful with that wrapper
Not throw tins o'er someone's wall
To generously take home ones' litter
Not leave it hidden - till autumn's fall

Graham R Dunn, North Walsham

SIZEWELL AT DUNWICH

The grey metallic dome of Sizewell
hangs over on the horizon ahead, like a great neoplasm
sprouting from a concrete man-made bed

The ruins of lost Dunwich lie buried deep,

beneath the silt and ashen sea, opaque and foaming,
like used dish water, stone churning with the hunger of
winter;
not the languid, wholesome crash of a sandy bay

No one swims on this beach

Sand Martins have burrowed in the eroding cliffs,
attracted by the warm cinnamon sand, ignoring the
warning signs:
'digging holes in the cliffs can be dangerous'

Trees have walked in the night, lie derailed, roots drinking
the sky;
brown bones, wormholed dry, tumble from cliff edge
cemeteries
exhumed with each graveyard cough

Lone men crouch in green shelters on the beach, silent
people
staring out to sea, evacuees of the sea bombed house
with the wallpaper laughing in the wind

A feeling of desolation and macabre contamination
breathes an unseen presence and an urgency to leave this
place

Vesuvius glows quietly in the distance

Nicola Scott, Bury St Edmunds

THE ETERNAL CITY

'The eternal city', Rome - the cliche's apt -
Or why would it be a cliche, a phrase
That gels and sticks, so congruously capped
It defies dilution or turgescence, plays

Its typecast part in the language, is trapped
And bled of novelty to granite greys
Of a monument - thus petrified the sapped
Given time, anything could be cliche'd,
Granted its irreducible thing, bare bone,
Something tied up which yet unfurls the braid
Of its own recurrence and redeems its drone,
Something whose uniqueness is its clone:
There's more to cliches than repetition -
They father new phrases by their fission

Peter Buckingham, Cambridge

ACROSS THE DUNES

A horizon structured out of sand-dunes and fond memo-
ries; of another time when the grass blazed white across
the hills, and dogs stalked fresh scents,
Young eyes stared out in to the brightly coloured distance,
Where nothing was explained and trees like canopies shel-
tered the eccentric pathways striding out in to our land-
scape

Laurence Calvert, Gt Yarmouth

KING'S LYNN - ANCIENT TOWN

On that great River Ouse of tides,
When Bishops came to Lynn,
And medieval fishermen in fragile boats
Sailed forth on river tides,
Out to the German Sea,
And ocean ships heavy with laden trade
That filled proud merchants purses
And John the King travelled here
To charter rich markets,
Rich in wares from everywhere

Then Bishop's Lynn lost that name,
And King's Lynn became a fact,
But still brave fisherfolk
Ride tides out to the Wash,
And merchantmen still find a dock
In King's Lynn ancient town
Where all the past is now

Richard Reeve, King's Lynn

AS HE SLEEPS

He lays there dead as night,
With showers teaming down,
Then wetting the ground,
As he sleeps so handsome so pure

His chest increases,
Then gives way,
To let some more air pass his way,
As he sleeps so handsome so pure

What he dreams
I'll never know

Rosalyn Tortice, Cromer

GOOD SMELLS

Goods smell!
S-t-r-e-t-c-h,
The door opens.... Good smell! Much stronger,
Very good smell, It's coming from Thingy

What is it? Same muddy shoes,
Same old jeans,

Same sleepy face,
Same old coat - coat
COAT
It's coming from the coat

I point my nose and fire

It ends up, with the rest of me just behind,
Nuzzling his coat pocket,
"Get off" He says, fixing my lead,
"Later, if you're good. Come on!"

Hmmm. Very good smell

Oops! There goes my nose again

Fixing itself to that pocket without me even noticing

"Get off, brute" he says

Rain, cold, mist, mud and Smelllll - what a great day!

Tim Morgan, Colby

North West

NIGHT HOLD

I stayed this once to see the night arrive
Was well prepared, twice wrapped, in bankside dell
To crouch and watch in stillness and tranquillity
With scent of primrose and azure harebell

Soft green of newborn beech leaves tinkled soundlessly
Against the parent ridges of vast trunk
Stood deep in bed of own sprung littering
From ancient times and many ages sunk

The curling 'caterpillars' of the bracken tips
Waiting, once again, for warmth of day
To stretch, uncurl and grow into the bright green fronds
And spend their summertime in sweet display

High unseen call of mountain curlew lifts my head
To pirouette of midge shaft-locked in sun
Late laggard rook hurries home to roost and then
Bright voice of forest robins' closing song

Beneath the western sky of yellow greying
The pipestrelles swing round in harmony
Against the eastern dark they disappear
But mark their presence with a tiny melody

All colours melt and merge to silhouette black
A sudden still as chill of night takes hold
Strata of pine freeze into ice grey dusk
This early summer day breaks promise and brings winter
cold

My dell a velvet place of darkness thick
My soul is lost and gone into the night
All is complete - as death will be -
Would I'm as ready for that darkness, and that light

But no! Not yet! I roll my body free
Not yet. Not now. Another dawn to greet
And taking torch I stumble from that cell for home
For home, and light, and warmth - calling sweet

Anne Clare, Todmorden

THE HERON

The heron waits.
Hermit of the waterways
By nature isolated,
Stone still and granite grey he stands,
A statue replicated

The heron hunts
His glass bead eyes
The water's prism rejecting,
Stare straight into the dark deep pool
At victims unsuspecting

The heron strikes
This fisher king
Scorns rod or line or reel,
A lightning thrust with rapier bill
Impales the silvery eel

The heron flies
On pendulum beat,
Head high and feather crested;
His avian cousins gaze in awe
And leave him unmolested

The heron sleeps
Those glass bead eyes
Now under opaque awning;

Does he dream of a fish rich stream
That waits for him at dawning?

David Walker, Barrowford, Nelson

ALL GONE

Our love was good we knew the score
But the hurt I felt when she closed the door
I watched her back as she walked away
Was that last year or the other day
A few stupid words and too much wine
Now never again will she ever be mine
Everything we shared has drifted away
Was that last year or the other day
So on I now wander like shifting sand
And think of the day she held my hand

Edmund Bradbury, Wilmslow

SUMMER'S END

The moon fell from the sky
The night that you left
And in darkness plunged the earth
It rained stars for eons
In icy coldness
I was stranded
My only company
A dagger in my heart
The world died that night
Love became unheard of
A thing of centuries ago
Almost forgotten, but not quite
When you left me
On that cold summers night

Jessica Pritchard, Warrington

MOTHER

My mother, is so fair, her eyes are so blue
But if you really knew
What my mother can do
She's miles away, but I don't care
Because in my heart we're never apart
The warmth and love, I have for her
Will stay in my mind
Forevermore

Anne McTavish, Ulverston

SHE JAGUAR

I watch it move through
The blanket of dark
I watch it stare as it will
Make it's start
I watch it stop and
Enjoy the sight
This rare opportunity
Is worth my time
I observe its glossy, shiny black coat
As it parades around
As if to gloat
"I've got you now, it will be a feast!"
But NO it will never be defeat
Think now that secret has been
Exposed to me!
What it's like to be close to
A creature like She
She will have my heart
But not my soul
And my spirit will be free
To caress the whole
Of Her glossy, black shiny coat

I will find myself happy and carefree
That I will have learnt
The untold of a creature called,
She

Caroline Peate, Runcorn

DEATH OF SUMMER, BIRTH OF HOPE

Suddenly the first golden leaf adorned my tree.
It glistened amber in the morning sun,
As October grew older and the days shorter,
I donned my coat to ward off the winter's bite.

Late September came and went without a whisper
But the new month charged in as some raging beast,
Loudly claiming that summer had gone,
Together with swallows long flown to warmer coasts.

And as the greylag heads southwards to his winter home,
The cold rain speckled on my window pane.
The north east wind blew hard until the droplets dried
And brown stalks everywhere transfigured the dying earth.

Birdsongs of the spring I hardly remember you now.
I pray living Spirit, lead me through these gloomy days
of dark clouds and rain filled skies,
With nights heavily laden with loneliness and despair.

No children's shouts of joy, no happy laughter.
Gone from these rooms now,
To never know what they might have learned
From this deteriorating book of logic which I own,

I threw it into a swirling river
And let the water lead me to the sea,
Where the salty brine swallowed my tears

And dried my eyes for ever.

Then I looked and saw the birth of a new day
When I would glow with an everlasting light.
The seasons changed no more
But lingered always springtime in a new born earth.

David Holland, St Helens

IMAGES

I saw it again last night!
Fleetingly, but so poignantly real
Yet unreal, like a dancing sprite
Something I wanted to touch and feel

It was so happy and carefree
I wanted to catch it I fear

I know it really belongs to me
But how could I so careless have been
To have lost something so very dear
Something that I long to redeem

At least I know now what it is
It visits me often in my dreams
It's the ghost of myself, A haunting kiss
A re-living of my memories

Joyce Sugarman, Winsford

THE STAR

Lamp of the night softly gleaming
Oe'r all the world and oe'r me
Star of the morning and evening
Star of the ocean and sea

When the twilight brings forth a stillness
And a hush can be heard oe'r the earth
A star shines in solitary splendour
An eye twinkling moment, gives birth

My star can be seen, looking westward
And as the night deepens, it goes
On the long, glorious journey, to eastward
And as the night wanes, it still glows

Then with the dawn of the morning
It shines forth, with a last golden spark
Vying sometimes with the sun's burst
A glimmer of hope in our dark

On mountains, in clear, crystal dawnings
I've seen the sun, moon and my star
My heart and my mind filled with beauty
I've had glimpses of Heaven afar

Jean Turner, Walton-le-Dale, Preston

FIRE

Wide eyed dogs watching
Listening keenly
As two sticks are rubbed
Frantically together

Promising themselves
To live alongside
This bold creature wrapped
in borrowed furs, making heat

From a safe distance
Bears, wolverines, cats
Slant-eyed in envy

See plans of hunting thwarted

Eager, hungrily
The pure flame soars up
Sending smoke tendrils
To search out more sustenance

Never conscious
That its makers have
By its possession
Become kings of creation

Joan Kelly, Prestwich

THE GATEWAY

The gateway to heaven
Is not very wide
If you lead a good life
And are honest and kind
You can go inside
If you've been a rogue and not without sin
You'll wait for the devil
To take you with him
The place that you go will be very hot
But you'll have to go
Like it or not
So if you want to walk through those pearly gates
Change your ways
Before it's too late

Joyce Leigh, Bury

YOUR BOOK OF LIFE

When you are born
Life is an empty book
With many pages to be filled
At the beginning you depend on

Others to write about your life
And make of it what they will
But as you grow and fill the pages
With experiences of your own
Sometimes happy, sometimes sad
You are your own person
Some chapters are long, and some are short
From first steps to schooldays
To teenage years and adulthood
Forever changing
and as you reach your twilight years
And you turn back the pages
With memories of yesteryear
You wonder where the story will end
And if anyone will remember
YOUR BOOK OF LIFE...

Marian Smith, Hensingham, Whitehaven

INOV "THE RED"

Seven yellows, seven reds and the black
To pot them you must have the knack
If your opponents missed you'll get a chance
To chalk your tip and get your stance
You pot one here you pot one there
There's one on the cush to try if you dare
One more yellow to sink in the middle
The ref calls a foul, it must be a fiddle
Up steps Inov with a sigh of relief
Robbed of my glory, he must be a thief
Foul yet again, the ref's a good chap
I get cheered on with a yell and a clap
Yellow's in, black's easy, cue's like lead
Down it goes, but I'm .. IN OFF THE RED ..

Paul Roberts, Southdene, Kirkby

I HEARD THE CRY OF FREEDOM

I heard the cry of freedom from far, far away
These people have no say
Because if they do
They are locked away
Day after day
They sit and pray
We are brothers and sisters
No matter where we live
It's compassion we must give
When I heard the cry of freedom
I thought my heart would break
It's their dignity and lives they take
When I kneel and pray
I hope there will come a day
When all governments can talk things through
So their suffering can end
Innocent people are bombed
In the name of a cause
So angels who are ordinary people we send
To let all nations and leaders see
Through a lot of hard work and trust
And understanding
We can have peace
And wars will cease
We heard your cries
And felt your pain
And one day we will gain
Freedom for all

Rita Sheldon, Lancaster

THE RIVER

White the torrent over rock and stone
Swirling eddies, creaming foam

Under the bank, a quiet pool
Where willow branches their tips do cool

A grassy bank, a summer flower
Sentinel trees whose branches tower
Flanking the stream on either hand
As it flows through this verdant land

The flash of a swallow from bank to bank
The gleam of white on a heron's flank
A kingfisher in brilliant blue
Add to the scene a glorious hue

A blend of light and shadow deep
Where the feeding fishes leap
Leaving ever widening rings
To the reeds where the cricket sings

Robert E Fraser, Burnley

CONTRASTS

Great cathedrals, so ornate,
Contrast the homeless at the gate.
Western tables full of food to eat,
Contrast the starving. Hearts stopping to beat.

Countries basking in joys of peace
Contrast the lands where wars never cease.
Precious freedom that people cherish
Contrast those countries where people perish.

Humans slain in senseless strife
Contrast those who savour sweet life.
Green fields scattered with mines that kill
Contrast ours where we roam at will.

Some enjoy peace on earth
Contrast those humans in terror since birth.

Welcome the roof over our heads
And the food we eat today.
Contrast Third World gutters
Where humans shrink and pass away.

Terry Coneys, Chorley

BEST FRIENDS

We are best friends, you know it's true
You always make me laugh, and never blue
You're firm, hard, loving and caring
Never tight fisted, you're always sharing
You tell your jokes with such delight
And I could laugh with you all night
Your chubby cheeks and cuddly tum
I know you're not a bum
You would give your last to me, I know
Our friendship can do nothing but glow
I'll always love you, till the day I die
Our friendship will continue, up in the sky
We will be friends, up there in heaven
I'll meet you mate, at golden gate seven

Susan Hindley, Boughton, Chester

RETIREMENT

It takes some time to realise
That time is all your own
And, getting used to having it
Something you've never known
No more early rising, no more morning rush
You can take your time at last, no-one makes a fuss

Out goes the alarm clock, get up when you like
Plan the day to do the things
You've dreamed of all your life
There's no-one giving orders
On what you have to do
Some people sit at home and 'mope'
They think their life is done
But if you've worked hard all those years
You've reached your goal, you've won
So every morn' when you awake
Be glad that you're alive
For each day is a holiday
No more 'Nine to Five'

Carmel Allison, Thornton Cleveleys

MEMORIES

I remember bopping
In dance halls Saturday night
Poppet beads and waspy belts
Bee hives, what a sight

I remember Teddy boys
Brylcream in their hair
Blue suede shoes and drainpipes
Playing truth or dare

I remember coloured stoles
Keeping out the cold
Cardigans, worn front to back
I must be getting old

I remember, pens with nibs
Ink pots in a hole
Coffee bars and record booths
Good old Rock and Roll

I remember all these things
Though it took me quite a while
I think it's done my memory good
And it made me smile

Eunice Lee, Wigan

THE LIFE OF RACHAEL BROWN

The day she was born, it rained all day
She used to hear her mother say
Never loved, treated like dirt
nobody knew how much it hurt
Always a lackey, her mother a whore
She hated the noises behind that door
At school they laughed and called her names
A lonely little girl so filled with shame
At junior school she ran away
No shoes on her feet nowhere to stay
As hunger set in, the pimps came near
They forced her into a life of fear
Used, abused, so empty inside
Nowhere to run, no place to hide
Then came the drugs, they helped set her free
Away from the ugliness of her misery
She took her own life at the age of fourteen
It was as if her life had never been
In the corner of the graveyard is a single stone
Written upon it NAME UNKNOWN

Janet Owens, Liverpool

North
East

THAT OLD FAMILIAR SONG

A lovely man was our Uncle Patrick
Quiet, moderate in every way
The only time he took a drink
Was on the eve of New Year's Day

Then after a couple of tots of the hard stuff
He would stand; after a bit of a push
And plaintively sing "Macushla"
With such yearning it turned us to mush.

As he sang of a love lost forever
His wife with her face full of doom
Would also stand, then swish her way
Disdainfully from the room

Our Aunt Nell was a beautiful woman
A lady and yet you could tell
When Uncle sang his old love song
He wasn't thinking about Auntie Nell.

Alice Longley, Wakefield

SINS

I see no reason to live,
We sit here and try to be nice to each other,
When hate fills up our hearts.

The emptiness grows within,
The eighth and most deadly sin,
The bitterness swells and the pain starts.

I have no reason to live,
I am born, I die, I give no contribution,
It may as well be ended as soon as it begins.

When I no longer live,
May I be as one with the earth, which from my birth
And death will gain only the pain and sins.

Ashleigh Fletcher, Sunderland

GET WELL SOON MUM

Mother Earth is suffering, in fact, she's very ill
Mother Earth is dying but we abuse her still
Consuming her resources and putting nothing back
Polluting the environment and forcing it off track
The ozone layer is gaping but no one seems to care
The forest fires keep raging creating desserts bare
Our roads are clogged with traffic spewing cancerous
fumes
From fossil burning engines each living thing consumes
The good book says that God chose man to take care of His
realm
And made him in His image then put him at the helm
Supposing man's intelligence would guide a concerned
mind
Towards care for other creatures some millions in kind
But every day a habitat by man's hand is destroyed
Another species disappears into the unknown void
To sate man's growing avarice for timber, oil, and gold
Till Mother Earth is groaning growing prematurely old
But what about the future and the children yet unborn
Shall we condemn them to a fate of flood and fire and
storm
Or should we stop and think now of how to turn the tide
Before we wake one morning to find that Mother Earth has
died.

Brian Denton, Morpeth

DANES DYKE

Late Autumn sun
reflecting the light

gold speckled brown
with chalky stone white
contrasts, at the dyke.

Beyond the horizon
the cameras roll.
Bobbing white horses.
Rough seas take their toll
in the cold winter chill.

Later on in the year
as we follow the trail,
daffodils and bluebells
bud without fail,
amid whipping March winds.

Wooded areas where tourists sunbathe
with the sea gently rippling
inviting the brave
to swim in the brine
where the Danes left their sign.

Carol Stubbs, Bridlington

ENDINGS

it's worse at night
and every night as i carefully
key in the magic number that will keep us safe
and climb to the tock, tock,
that will last to the top stair -
i remcmber

i find the purple heart pull
the light snaps on -
glancing behind the bathroom door
i remember your folded clothes
your neatness i admired,
the clothes are still folded but now

remnants in pine drawers.

looking up from our carved king sized bed
i see your dark face
when your bareness filled the room
and we clung helpless in our love

i set the clock to ring loudly
and when it rings
my already awake body lurches towards the window -
our window - our sunday morning teacup
picture window
and i remember.

Cathy Chadwick, Mexborough

THE ALLOTTED SPAN

What do we do with this time given,
Do we stumble thro' life with never a care
Or do we use it sometimes to pause and stare
Of all the bustle and worry around
Do we look up, or do we look down.
Look, see the daffodil in spring
Nodding its head, its message to bring
The peace, we all so dearly want
Instead of do this, do that, and don't!
We are lucky, to live our allotted span
To love, to need, do things we can
Some do not make it, in youth they are taken
Others are lost, hungry and forsaken
Life is soft, or hard, whatever we make it
But is not all toil and tears and having to fake it!
Life is a circle, that's everlasting
A series of rounds, fed in one life, or fasting
Whatever we do with this, our time
To do ones best with love, is divine.

E Lawson, Pontefract

MORE RAIN...

At this point in time,
My eyes can only see rain.
Not through stinging tears
Of sadness or joy.
But eyes that are clouded
By mist hazy memories.

Memories of places
That we visited once.
Memories of faces
Never to be seen again.
Memories of events
In which we took part.
Memories of loved ones
Still within my heart.

Will the sun appear again
And clear the mist,
So that my thoughts become clear
And I can focus once more
On the love we shared
Before the rain...

George Thomas, South Shields

THE LOST ALCHERINGA

Rachel found me in a slow and dreamy way
Like a memory growing dull in a haze of time
And I squinted up through the glare and sorry sky
Saw her falling like an evening's longing shadow
What was that feeling now, they ask in dusk grey
It's a struggle to recall any memory of mine
She drew the curtains again leaving my head dry
And my eyes closed to grasp what was gone with the
night...

...A spinning camera shot of cornfields and glare
See-through sea horses and bullet soaked arms...
What is it you saw there before the dawn invasion
The charge of the light and the   retinas?
Attempts to recapture and rescue the night's air
Before it sinks forever with the flares and alarms
Fail under the dark storm of daybreak and bleached vision
Has it gone now again, was it scared by the light?

Farewell my invisible sygnathidaes
Back again they vanish and I am left to stumble
I watch the opening sky break above my bed
And can just make out the clouds in hippocampus shapes
The sleep gets washed from the day blinded eyes
By the resonant sounds of Rachel's morning mumble
Clear out the final straggling dream strands from my head
They are gone again, as the night wings away in flight.

James Wilkinson, Harrogate

THE VALE OF PICKERING

The heat of day drains slowly from the sun-warmed stones,
While overhead the hunting swallows cry.
A soft mist settles gently over distant fields
As evening casts its net along the sky.

Across the vale, a lantern in the greying gloom,
Some other home its welcome glimmer sheds.
The night sinks, sighing, to the pillowed land
And weary souls go gladly to their beds.

Jean Oxley, Scarborough

IN MEMORY OF LOVE

The flowers that I lay above you will die
as you have died, and their life as your
life will cease to grow, their beauty will

fade like this day will fade, as tideless
as the years that come and go,

but the love I have for you will not die
as you have died, for with you it lies at
peace and free of pain, till with death I
come and sleep with thee, that we may
share our dreams again,

When once more will we live those yester
years, of a time our love was young, a time
when neath the stars we lay, for our world
had just begun, for 'twas then eternal vows
we made, that time could never break, till
came the day you closed your eyes, never
more to see them wake,

Please now my love while you sleep, let your
dreaming be always of me,
for while I live my love, will my memories
be always of thee,

Jim Cuthbert, York

MOTHER

What do you do with a mother's things
After a mother is dead?
Not the bracelets, and rings, and strings
Of pearls, but the small unvalued things

What do you do with a mother's dresses
After a mother is dead?
Hanging there in the wardrobe presses,
They are part of her, her pretty dresses

What do you do with a mother's shoes
After a mother is dead?

Shoes that maybe you helped her choose
Soft little empty cared for shoes

What do you do with a mother's brush and comb
After a mother is dead?
What can you do with her home
And her loss, and her love, and her brush and comb

Joan Firth, Pudsey

MAN'S BEST FRIEND

A rock I am to lean on, a friend so true and fair
I'm covered from head to toe in hairy, hairy, hair
In darkness I'll walk with you, be always by your side
I'll guard you from intruders, be your eyes if you are blind
And yet they still abuse me, and beat me with a stick
They really don't deserve me, they really make me stick

I have been with man since time began and since he
learned to talk
I'll fetch a stick you throw for me, if you take me a walk

So you must learn to give to me
The kindness I deserve
Treat me well new master, and you I'll always serve

Leigh J Arkwright, Barnsley

WHAT IS CHRISTMAS?

What is Christmas?
A flurry of lists and buying cards
The hiding of bulky packages
In unlikely places
Children's eager faces

Is it -

The scent of spices, cinnamon and cloves
Richness from the kitchen
The house decked with holly?

Or is it -

Those quiet moments while we wait
Our breath curling above us in the cold air
To hear again the well loved story
We stand to join the youthful voices
Singing of shepherds and angels in glory
To balance our need against our greed
And remember the child in a simple stable

Mary Found, Knaresborough

OH, THE MASK THAT PEOPLE WEAR

She walks in isolated splendour, prominent position in
the community, pillar of respectability. Good job, nice
house, grown up family - OH, THE MASK THAT PEOPLE
WEAR!

For in truth she walks alone. Her thoughts, her feelings,
are desperate in the whirlpool of her despair - OH, THE
MASK THAT PEOPLE WEAR!

"She's so kind, so thoughtful, isn't she? She'll do anything
you ask. She's so happy, so carefree, always has a smile"! -
OH, THE MASK THAT PEOPLE WEAR!

For in reality she cries alone.
Her solitude is deep and her wounds are old.
She prays for someone just to share - OH, THE MASK
THAT PEOPLE WEAR!

Vonny Holloway, Sheffield

DREAM LAND

The warmth of the dark green forest,
the sound of the trickling stream

Am I walking in the countryside,
or is it just a dream?

All the birds are singing,
the sun is shining bright

But is this early morning,
or the middle of the night?

Life just seems so wonderful,
so peaceful and ideal

These things I have imagined,
for a moment seemed so real

Then everything became so clear,
Those heavenly thoughts were true

Half past six, the alarm bell rang,
and I woke up next to you!

Matthew Norcliffe, Skipton

SEPTEMBER LOVE

So many thought our love, like lust, would cool,
That time would prove the folly of our dream;
Too old to play the adolescent fool,
Just drift along in life's indifferent stream.

Regrets, we knew, would haunt our later years
If, letting fall this precious final chance,
We bent the knee to nagging doubts and fears,
"If onlys" clouding every backward glance.

Nine joyous years have proved our hearts knew best
And each has passed more quickly than the last;
Still shared excitement stirs within our breast
At joys to come and memories of those past.

But even nine more years and then yet nine
Could not exhaust the bliss that's yours and mine.

Philip Cook, Ripon

GRANTED

Take me for granted
Think you own me
Think you have a right over me
Think you can physically abuse me, scar me

Take me for granted
Tell me what to do
Tell me how to do it
Tell me when to do it

Take me for granted
Tell me I'm no good
Tell me I'm useless
Tell me I'm worthless

Take me for granted
Abuse my love
Abuse my body
Abuse my mind

Take me for granted
For how long
Until I'm gone

Saiqah Salim, Bradford

YORKSHIRE FOLK

Yorkshire folk have a great deal of sense,

They are taught early on to "look after the pence"
Don't spend a bob when a tanner will do,
They may change the names but the feelings run true

Why do the southerners think we are thick
Owt 'North of Watford comes in for some stick

Could be because they can't tell what we say,
Broad Yorkshire they'll never get, try as they may

Eye, don't think we're stupid 'cos flat caps we wear
There's brains under them caps, and not just our hair

We care for each other through thick and through thin,
If you come to Yorkshire you'll find we 'muck in'

There's thousands of phrases folks won't understand,
but no place like YORKSHIRE - the best in the land!

Sheila M Gannon, Leeds

CONTEMPLATION

So many people from my yesterdays lay their hold on me
I find that I belong, not to myself alone, but merge with
Loved ones gone before, merge as one or many, I cannot
tell
My heart and mind and memory hold part of each departed
one
Fast in the bonds of love and kinship, each day I see them
Mirrored in my face and form, the way I think and feel
The values they instilled in me, their heritage from others
gone before
I pray, I tarnish not the faith they placed in me, and pass it
on
To those to whom I joyfully have given life.

A Gillmeister, Selby

Scotland

KISS OF DEATH

By death you've been kissed...
Fear that you won't be missed
Now this is no lie
When it's your turn to die
Evade if you can
You'll have walked you'll have ran
But you'll feel lower
Find that you'll run slower
Till life brings you down
In your fav'rite home town
Few words from your boss
Of his factory's loss
Knowledge within you
Says work will continue
With new hands and wrists
Like you didn't exist
For you won't be missed...
since by death you've been kissed

Bill Chapman, Dumbarton

HOPE SPRINGS ETERNAL

The lottery and scratch-cards,
Horses, Bingo and the pools,
People parting with their money,
Why, oh why, are they such fools?

The answer's very simple.
In this time of deep recession
A harmless little flutter
Helps to combat their depression.

For one optimistic moment
They can let their dreams run riot.
Whoever wants whatever,

They could just go out buy it.

All too soon comes cold reality
With all its stress and strife,
And they're back to that biggest gamble of all -
The lottery of life!

Dorothy White, Whitecrook, Clydebank

OLD FATHER TIME

Old Father Time
Nears with his scythe
Keening the wind
In search of a life

I've lived like a tree
Steady and strong
My loved ones round me
How long for how long

I hear his call
In my tortuous sleep
Give me your all
And enter my keep

But like the tree
Heavy with fruit
Two lives or more
Will stem from one root

And now my leaves
No longer green
Will drift through lives
Their, caring, unseen

And my branches will smile
Full of song and laughter

And maybe some while
They'll think of their Father

Old Father Time confound you to Hell

James Miller Watt, Aberdeen

FALLEN ANGELS

We wandered, my son, and I
Past fallen angels, faces carved in stone
Their sightless eyes, greened with age
Smiled kindly upon man and boy
Oblivious to love, blind to joy
Seeing not the gathering gloom
Or the child's' hand, holding my own
Nor the decay of neglect around them, strewn

Realms of destruction sown, by a human hand
Beauty, blighted by stupid youth
Alone the cupids and the angels stand
Blind to brutality, indifferent to truth
A place of peace, marble and stone
Father and son, flesh and blood
The angels, and us, we stand alone

Now dusk was falling, we quickened our pace
Passed petrified flowers, the scent of decay
The leaves rustled softly in the gentle breeze
The rusting gate closed, and night followed day

Scott Martin, Dundee

DRIVING HIM CRAZY

During some of my near misses in the street
My Driving Instructor wishes he had an ejector seat
he used to have an attitude of come what may
Now he has taken up religion in a serious way

Praying that I get to grips with the clutch
instead of emulating the driving of Starsky and Hutch
i don't think I've won his confidence so far
As he's tried shouting instructions from outside the car
he used to take all his lessons in his stride
now he insists the drivers airbag is on his side
With me he has viewed some sights never seen
Especially with his face that close to the windscreen
He said that my driving is making him insane
Recently he's went from Valium to Cocaine
He said he'll be happy when I sit my test
For he is admitting himself to hospital for a rest
Then he said something that I didn't like
"Ever thought about lessons for a motorbike"
After I had time to get over the initial shock
I've discovered it would be cheaper and safer just to walk

Thomas M Bell, Kilsyth, Glasgow

A MEMORY FROM 1940

When I first tried on my brand new "Duds"
What a problem I had with front and back studs
And even more with those blinking cuff links
This dressing up caper? In my view "It Stinks"

Fighting hours with that darned starched collar
Three streets away, they could hear me holler
Shoes with a shine you could see your face in
Finally I was ready, shining like a new pin

I felt heads would turn, once I stepped outside
Sure I was immaculate, my pride I couldn't hide
But I was shattered, as my pals gave a hoot
At the sight of me, (a twelve year old) in
My first long trousered suit

W Winton, Wester Hailes, Edinburgh